THE STORY OF THE TORONTO RAPTORS

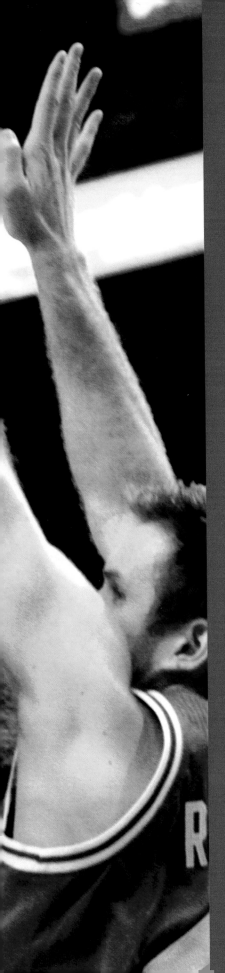

THE NBA:
A HISTORY
OF HOOPS

THE STORY OF THE
TORONTO
RAPTORS

NATE FRISCH

CREATIVE EDUCATION · CREATIVE PAPERBACKS

Published by Creative Education and Creative Paperbacks
P.O. Box 227, Mankato, Minnesota 56002
Creative Education and Creative Paperbacks are imprints
of The Creative Company
www.thecreativecompany.us

Design and production by Blue Design
Art direction by Rita Marshall
Printed in the United States of America

Photographs by Corbis (REBECCA COOK/Reuters, Chris
Faytok/Star Ledger, CHRIS KEANE/Reuters, JUSTIN
LANE/epa, FRED THORNHILL/Reuters, Underwood
& Underwood), Getty Images (Nathaniel S. Butler/
NBAE, Gary Dineen/NBAE, Ned Dishman/NBAE, Jeremy
Edwards, Barry Gossage/NBAE, Andy Hayt/NBAE,
Jed Jacobsohn, Craig Jones, Steve Lipofsky, Fernando
Medina/NBAE, NBA Photo Library/NBAE, David Sherman/
NBAE, Ron Turenne/NBAE, Phil Walter), Newscom (Albert
Pena/Icon SMI, USA TODAY Sports (RVR)

Library of Congress Cataloging-in-Publication Data
Frisch, Nate.
The story of the Toronto Raptors / Nate Frisch.
p. cm. — (The NBA: a history of hoops)
Includes index.
Summary: An informative narration of the Toronto Raptors
professional basketball team's history from its 1995
founding to today, spotlighting memorable players and
reliving dramatic events.
ISBN 978-1-60818-449-1 (hardcover)
ISBN 978-1-62832-035-0 (pbk)
1. Toronto Raptors (Basketball team)—History—Juvenile
literature. I. Title.

GV885.52.T67F758 2014
796.323'6409713541—dc23   2013039667

CCSS: RI.5.1, 2, 3, 8; RH.6-8.4, 5, 7

PBK 9 8 7 6 5 4 3 2

Cover: Guard DeMar DeRozan
Page 2: Guard Kyle Lowry
Pages 4-5: Center Jonas Valanciunas
Page 6: Forward Antonio Davis

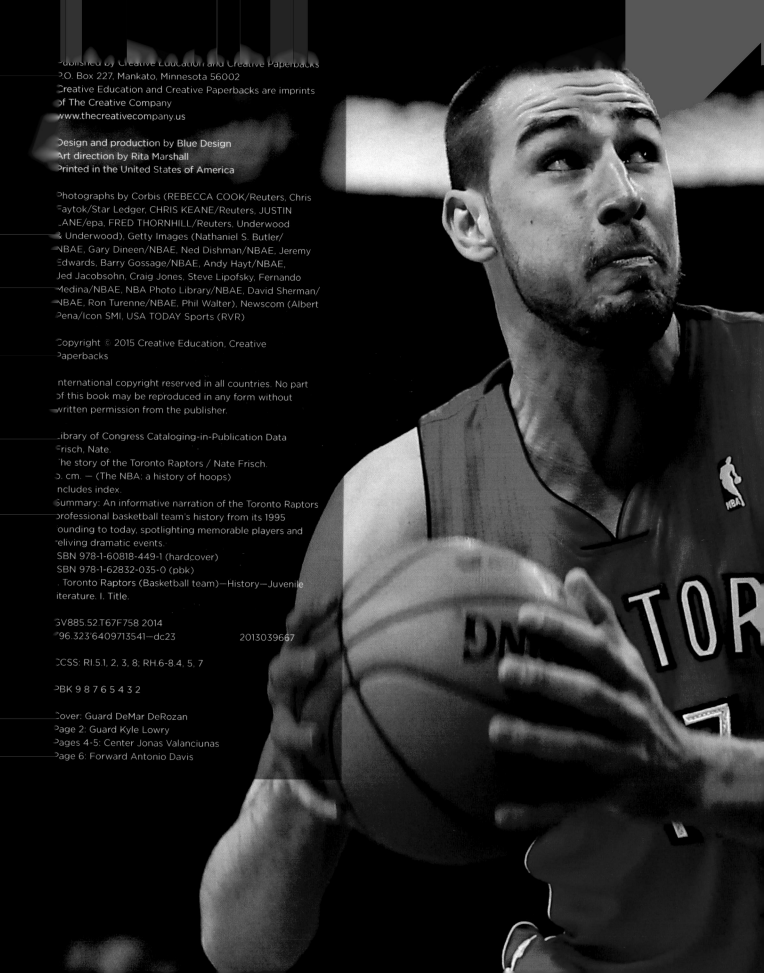

TABLE OF CONTENTS

COURTSIDE STORIES

INTRODUCING...

CANADA WELCOMES THE NBA

TORONTO'S ROGERS CENTRE STADIUM AND CN TOWER WERE BUILT NEAR LAKE ONTARIO.

T oronto, Ontario, sits on the north shore of Lake Ontario, which forms a natural boundary between Canada and the United States. It was founded in the late 1700s by the British, who wanted land along the important waterway but had recently lost their American claims following the Revolutionary War. Over the past two centuries, the city had attracted immigrants from many other countries as well, and Toronto swelled to become Canada's most populous city. In sharp contrast to the Canadian wilderness perception, the Toronto cityscape combines impressive historic structures and modern skyscrapers, and the CN Tower, the world's sixth-tallest freestanding structure, makes for an unmistakable skyline. Today, the diverse city exhibits a mixture of financial, technological, and artistic flair.

Toronto is also Canada's most diverse city in terms of

TORONTO STRENGTHENED ITS ROSTER WITH SEASONED VETERANS SUCH AS GUARD WILLIE ANDERSON.

sports franchises. The history of the beloved Maple Leafs of the National Hockey League (NHL) dates back to 1917, and the Blue Jays of Major League Baseball have called Toronto home since 1977. The city has also hosted pro football, soccer, and lacrosse clubs over the years. In 1993, more spice was added to an already varied sports scene when the National Basketball Association (NBA) decided to expand into Canada and awarded the city a franchise. The new club asked Torontonians to select the team name, and the winning entry was Raptors—a reference to swift, predatory dinosaurs that wielded deadly claws.

Businessman John Bitove was the franchise's first owner, and he had about two years to build up an organization that would begin competing in 1995. He chose former Detroit Pistons star Isiah Thomas as vice president of basketball operations. Thomas then hired former Pistons assistant coach Brendan Malone as the Raptors' head coach. While in Detroit, the two had enjoyed back-to-back NBA titles in 1989 and 1990. The Pistons of that era were known as the "Bad Boys" for their toughness and win-at-all-costs nature. Thomas and Malone hoped to bring that attitude to Toronto. "We know as an expansion team we may not have a lot of

BASKETBALL: MADE IN CANADA

Around the world, most fans of basketball believe the sport finds its origins in the United States. While it's true that the game's founder, James Naismith, is credited with inventing basketball while living in Springfield, Massachusetts, in 1891, what most people do not know is that Naismith was Canadian. Born in a small township near Almonte, Ontario, Naismith grew up to be a fine athlete, competing in collegiate football, soccer, and gymnastics. After graduating from Montreal's McGill University, he moved to the U.S. to take a job as a physical education teacher at a YMCA in Springfield. Asked by his boss to invent an indoor game to "provide an athletic distraction" for his unruly students, Naismith came up with the sport he called Basket Ball. The original game featured 13 basic rules and bore only a basic resemblance to today's sport, but Naismith's students grew to love it, and the game's popularity expanded quickly. More than a century later, millions around the world enjoy the graceful, athletic game of basketball, and it's all thanks to one of Canada's favorite sons.

DAMON STOUDAMIRE

POSITION GUARD
HEIGHT 5-FOOT-10
RAPTORS SEASONS
1995–98

At 5-foot-10 and 171 pounds, Damon Stoudamire did not fit the usual description of a franchise player in the NBA. In a league dominated by giants, the comparatively diminutive Stoudamire proved that a smaller player could not only contribute but could actually excel. Stoudamire had heard the criticism about his size his entire life, but after enjoying a stellar college career at the University of Arizona, he was no longer worried about what others said. In fact, as a child, Stoudamire's favorite cartoon character was Mighty Mouse, who, despite being small, was famous for saving the day. "Mighty Mouse" eventually became Stoudamire's nickname, and after the expansion Toronto Raptors made him their very first draft pick, he quickly became the team's hero. During his rookie season, Stoudamire used his blazing speed and deadly shooting touch to average 19 points and 9.3 assists per game—good enough to earn the 1996 Rookie of the Year award. Throughout his career in Toronto, Stoudamire remained the focal point of the team and the face of the new franchise.

"WE KNOW AS AN EXPANSION TEAM WE MAY NOT HAVE A LOT OF OFFENSIVE WEAPONS, BUT WE CAN CREATE OFFENSE WITH TOUGH DEFENSE, AND WE WILL PLAY TOUGH DEFENSE EVERY NIGHT."

– COACH BRENDAN MALONE

offensive weapons," said Malone. "But we can create offense with tough defense, and we will play tough defense every night."

Toronto's first step in building its roster came via an expansion draft, where it selected existing NBA players made available by their former teams. No team offered up great stars, of course, but the Raptors did stockpile some size by choosing centers Oliver Miller and Zan Tabak, and power forward Sharone Wright. They also added tall, athletic, defensive-minded guard Doug Christie. Then, in the 1995 NBA Draft, the Raptors selected 5-foot-10 point guard Damon Stoudamire from the University of Arizona with the seventh overall pick. Some NBA teams were turned off by Stoudemire's small stature, but Thomas—who compiled a Hall-of-Fame career at a height of only 6-foot-1—admired the young guard's leadership, speed, passing, and deadly shooting touch.

In November 3, 1995, the Raptors played their first game, defeating the New Jersey Nets 94–79 at home in Toronto's SkyDome. Even with the promising start, wins would be scarce that first season as the Raptors posted a 21–61 record. Win or lose, Raptors fans were thrilled by the play of Stoudamire, whose steady average of 19 points and 9.3 assists per game earned him the NBA Rookie of the Year award.

Before the 1996–97 season, Thomas made a coaching change, replacing Malone with Darrell Walker. In the Draft, Toronto chose versatile forward Marcus Camby with its first-round pick. The 6-foot-11 Camby gave the Raptors an athletic big man to complement the gifted Stoudamire. Sparked by its two young stars, Toronto's record improved to 30–52, and the future looked bright. "We're young and we're still learning," said Raptors guard Doug Christie. "But we're getting better, and pretty soon, maybe we'll be giving the lessons."

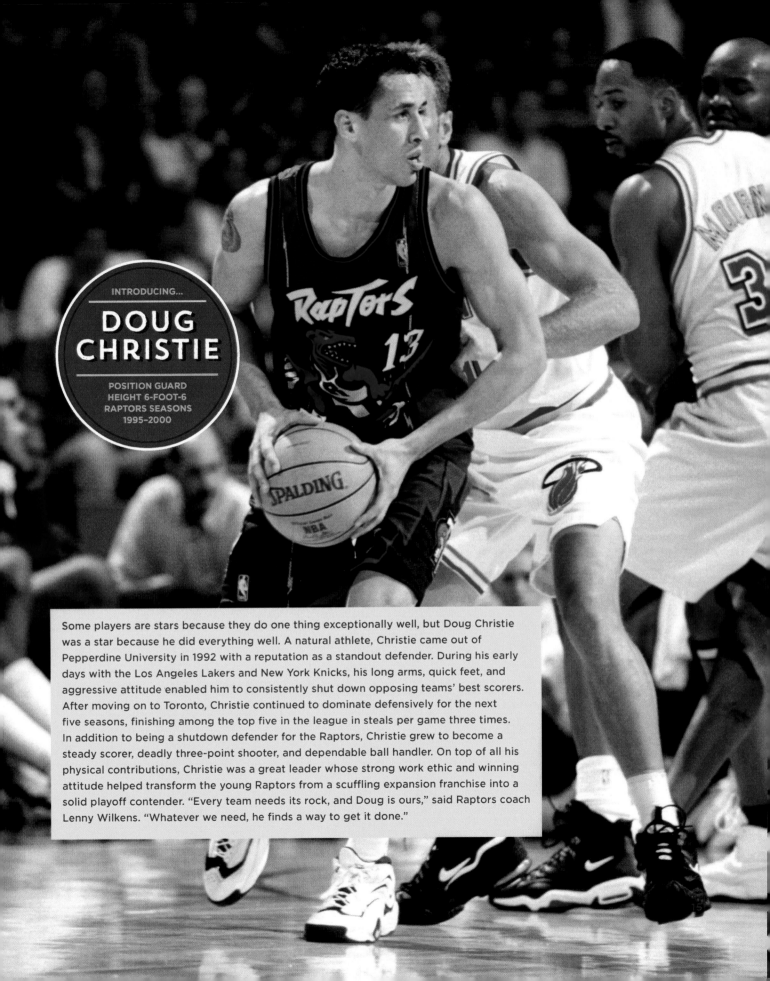

INTRODUCING...

DOUG CHRISTIE

POSITION GUARD
HEIGHT 6-FOOT-6
RAPTORS SEASONS
1995–2000

Some players are stars because they do one thing exceptionally well, but Doug Christie was a star because he did everything well. A natural athlete, Christie came out of Pepperdine University in 1992 with a reputation as a standout defender. During his early days with the Los Angeles Lakers and New York Knicks, his long arms, quick feet, and aggressive attitude enabled him to consistently shut down opposing teams' best scorers. After moving on to Toronto, Christie continued to dominate defensively for the next five seasons, finishing among the top five in the league in steals per game three times. In addition to being a shutdown defender for the Raptors, Christie grew to become a steady scorer, deadly three-point shooter, and dependable ball handler. On top of all his physical contributions, Christie was a great leader whose strong work ethic and winning attitude helped transform the young Raptors from a scuffling expansion franchise into a solid playoff contender. "Every team needs its rock, and Doug is ours," said Raptors coach Lenny Wilkens. "Whatever we need, he finds a way to get it done."

DUNCAN 8

A. FOYLE 15

VAN HORN 9

T. McGRADY 16

BILLUPS 10

17

DANIELS

18

ATTIE 19

20

THE RAPTORS RETOOL

HIGH SCHOOL STANDOUT TRACY McGRADY SAW LIMITED PLAYING TIME AS A ROOKIE.

OMAS 14

21

Prior to the 1997–98 season, Toronto continued to add young talent through the NBA Draft, using its first-round pick on 18-year-old swingman Tracy McGrady from Mount Zion Christian Academy in North Carolina. Although he came to the league directly from high school, McGrady's physical gifts were impossible to ignore. At 6-foot-8, he boasted a 42-inch vertical leap and was a superb ball handler. "He'll need to develop his shot and grow some man muscles to compete against the kind of athlete he's going to see in the NBA," said then Chicago Bulls coach Phil Jackson. "But there is no doubt, if he puts in the work, he'll be a star in this league."

Unfortunately for McGrady and the Raptors, 1997–98 proved to be a disaster. Early on, injuries to key players such as Camby and forwards Walt Williams and Carlos Rogers led to a 17-game losing streak that effectively

TRACY McGRADY

POSITION FORWARD / GUARD
HEIGHT 6-FOOT-8
RAPTORS SEASONS
1997–2000

Most teenage boys only dream of successfully competing against NBA greats, but when Tracy "T-Mac" McGrady was chosen by Toronto with the ninth overall pick in the 1997 NBA Draft, it was apparent that he was not going to be the average teenager. Despite being only 1 month past his 18th birthday, McGrady possessed skills that were advanced beyond his years. His long body, excellent ball-handling skills, and explosive speed and leaping ability convinced scouts he would be a future star. While McGrady's skills and athleticism were NBA-ready right away, his strength and maturity needed time to develop. The Raptors used him carefully during his first two seasons, allowing him to become accustomed to the league's speed and physical play, but by his third season, McGrady began to flash his superstar potential. Teaming up with his distant cousin Vince Carter, McGrady helped lead the Raptors to the franchise's first postseason appearance in 2000. "Watching T-Mac is like watching a young musical prodigy," said teammate Dell Curry. "He does things naturally that the rest of us can only dream about."

ended the season before it began. Adding further turmoil, an ownership change during the middle of the season alienated Thomas. Upset that he was not given a larger ownership share and disappointed with the team's performance, Thomas resigned.

fter Thomas's departure, the Raptors decided to move away from his philosophy of building with youth. Toronto traded Stoudamire, Williams, and Rogers to the Portland Trail Blazers for guard Alvin Williams, two other players, and three future draft picks. The team also replaced Coach Walker with Butch Carter. The changes did not lead to victories, though, and the Raptors finished the season with a dismal 16–66 record. That summer, Camby was traded to the New York Knicks for veteran forward Charles Oakley.

Going into the 1998–99 season, the Raptors were looking for a player who could energize the franchise. With its first-round pick in the 1998 NBA Draft, Toronto chose forward Antawn Jamison, and then traded him to the Golden State Warriors for the rights to rookie forward/guard Vince Carter. The 6-foot-6 Carter was a great fit for the struggling Raptors. His explosive first step, incredible leaping ability, and knack for producing jaw-dropping highlights promised to bring new excitement and energy to a team that sorely needed it. Toronto fans were excited to see how Carter and McGrady, who were distant cousins, would do on the floor together. Their debut was delayed by a 4-month labor dispute between NBA owners and players that shortened the season to 50 games, but once play began in February,

the young duo led the Raptors to a respectable 23–27 mark. Carter's averages of 18.3 points and 5.7 rebounds per game opened eyes around the league and earned him the Rookie of the Year award. The season also marked the Raptors' move to their new home—the beautiful Air Canada Centre.

Encouraged by the team's improvement, Raptors management decided to add some veteran leadership to assist their developing stars. Prior to the 1999–2000 season, the team traded that year's first-round draft pick, forward Jonathan Bender, to the Indiana Pacers for forward Antonio Davis. The 6-foot-9 and 220-pound Davis matched with powerful frontcourt mates Oakley and center Kevin Willis to give Toronto the defense, rebounding, and strength it had lacked in the past. With the addition of other veterans such as sharpshooting guard Dell Curry, the Raptors took another step forward. Led by Carter and McGrady's combined 41.1 points per game and Davis and Oakley's combined 15.6 rebounds, the Raptors soared to the first winning campaign in team history, posting a 45–37 record and clinching their first playoff berth.

In the first round of postseason play, Toronto drew the powerful Knicks. Each game in the best-of-five series proved to be a close defensive struggle, with no contest decided by more than seven points. But the deeper, more experienced Knicks swept the Raptors in three straight games. "It's a tough blow to take after the season we had," said Carter. "We've got nothing to be ashamed of, though. We gave it all we had."

TORONTO'S FIRST TEAM

Most people believe the history of professional basketball in Canada began when the Toronto Raptors and Vancouver Grizzlies began league play in 1995. But the truth is, Toronto's NBA roots reach all the way back to 1946. That year, the Basketball Association of America (BAA) was founded, with the Toronto Huskies among its 11 original teams. The first game in BAA history featured the Huskies playing host to the New York Knickerbockers on November 1, 1946, before a crowd of 7,090 fans at Toronto's Maple Leaf Gardens. Toronto lost that first game and many others that season to finish with a record of 22–38, tied for last place with the Boston Celtics in the league's Eastern Division. Troubled by money problems and dwindling attendance, the Huskies folded after that initial season, but the BAA went on for two more years before merging with the National Basketball League (NBL) in 1949 to become the NBA. More than 60 years later, the NBA still regards the Huskies' 68–66 loss to the Knickerbockers as the first game in league history.

HALL OF FAME LEADERSHIP

LENNY WILKENS BELIEVED UNSELFISH PLAY AND TEAMWORK WOULD LEAD TO SUCCESS.

A fter that encouraging season, the Raptors' hopes for continued improvement were dealt a blow when McGrady was shipped to the Orlando Magic in 2000 for a first-round draft pick. As McGrady's skills had developed, it had become apparent that his natural position was shooting guard, the same as Carter. Finding it increasingly difficult to play in Carter's growing shadow, McGrady had requested a trade, and fearing that he would leave via free agency, the team obliged. The Raptors also made a coaching change, bringing in Lenny Wilkens to replace Butch Carter. Wilkens, one of only three people to be named to the Pro Basketball Hall of Fame as both a player and a coach, had a coaching resumé that included an NBA title with the Seattle SuperSonics in 1979 and more than 1,000 career victories. The Raptors front office brought the

HOME OF THE RAPTORS

What the Toronto Raptors' first home lacked in style, it made up for in seating. When the Raptors began play in 1995, they held their home games at SkyDome (now known as the Rogers Centre). The enormous domed stadium provided a spacious setting for the Raptors, with seating for 28,708 fans. Unfortunately, because the stadium was designed for baseball and football, the sight lines for basketball were poor, and the fans' cheers seemed to evaporate inside the cavernous facility. In 1999, the Raptors finally moved into a proper new home, the Air Canada Centre. Named after its airline sponsor, the arena was a major upgrade over SkyDome. Its 19,800 seats, state-of-the-art scoreboard, and fan-friendly facilities brought the game closer to the fans and allowed the Raptors to enjoy a definite home-court advantage. "We packed a lot of people in at SkyDome, but we never heard them," noted forward Vince Carter. "Now, at Air Canada, we know our fans are behind us." Nicknamed "The Hangar," the Air Canada Centre has provided a home to some of the NBA's greatest and most frequent fliers.

veteran coach aboard to push the rising team to the next level. "Lenny is a championship-caliber coach, and we think we are ready to contend," said Toronto guard Alvin Williams.

Given a leadership role under Wilkens, Carter took his game to new heights, averaging 27.6 points, 5.5 rebounds, and 3.9 assists per game. His acrobatic flights to the basket led to his earning the nickname "Half-Man/Half-Amazing." The team also benefited from the strong play of rookie forward Morris Peterson, whose outside shooting helped open up the floor for Carter. Driven by the dynamic play of their star, the Raptors posted a 47–35 record and earned another berth in the postseason.

In the first round, Toronto again faced the

MORRIS PETERSON (#24) AND GUARD FRED JONES (#20) TRIED TO HOLD THEIR GROUND.

25

VINCE GOES FOR 51

Vince Carter did many amazing things during his time in Toronto. The gravity-defying forward/guard was a highlight machine, and fans around the league came out in droves to see what he would do next. On February 27, 2000, Carter put on a show in the Air Canada Centre that would find its way into the record books. That night, Carter and the Raptors hosted the Phoenix Suns. Using an eye-popping variety of moves, including dunks, turnaround jumpers, and long-range bombs from behind the three-point line, Carter exploded for a Raptors-record 51 points in Toronto's 103–102 victory over the Suns. For the game, Carter was 17 of 32 from the field, including 4 of 8 from three-point range, but perhaps his most impressive feat of the night was the least spectacular—he was 13 of 13 from the free-throw line, with several coming near the game's end to clinch the victory for Toronto. "Vince was incredible," said Raptors guard Dee Brown. "He made so many tough shots against a good team in pressure situations—he just willed us to a win."

Knicks. New York won 2 out of the first 3 games to put Toronto on the brink of elimination, but Carter's 32- and 27-point explosions in Games 4 and 5 pushed the Raptors to a series victory. In the second round, Toronto faced the Philadelphia 76ers. After splitting the first six games of the series, it all came down to Game 7. With time running out and the Raptors down by one point, Carter's last-second shot missed, and Toronto lost the deciding game 88–87. "We rode Vince all the way here, and when that last shot of his left his hand, I thought we were going to advance," said Davis. "It didn't go down. That's basketball."

Before the next season, the Raptors added another big name when they acquired 39-year-old center Hakeem Olajuwon from the Houston Rockets. The team knew the 12-time All-Star was no longer the player he had been in his prime, but it hoped he could still contribute enough to push Toronto to the NBA Finals. Unfortunately, bad luck followed the Raptors throughout 2001–02. After posting a solid 29–21 start, Toronto fizzled when Carter

suffered a knee injury, which eventually led to a season-ending surgery. Finishing with a 42–40 mark, the Raptors qualified for the playoffs but lost a tough, five-game series to the Pistons to end the season.

VINCE CARTER

POSITION FORWARD / GUARD
HEIGHT 6-FOOT-6
RAPTORS SEASONS
1998–2004

There have been many highflying stars in the history of the NBA, but few flew as high as Vince Carter. The man nicknamed "Air Canada" and "Half-Man/Half-Amazing" brought energy and excitement to the young Toronto franchise with his mind-boggling dunks and scoring binges. After winning the Rookie of the Year award in 1999, Carter opened even more eyes when he won the NBA Slam Dunk Contest during the 2000 All-Star Game weekend festivities. Capable of incredible aerial acrobatics, Carter seemed to defy gravity when he launched himself toward the basket. His thunderous dunks filled highlight films, and his ability to take over a game offensively was reminiscent of another former University of North Carolina great, Michael Jordan. A five-time All-Star while in Toronto, Carter helped transform the young franchise into a perennial playoff contender. The excitement created by Carter's play even earned its own nickname—"Vinsanity." In Carter's career with Toronto, he scored 40 or more points in a game 12 times and broke the 50-point barrier once. In 2014, he stood as the franchise's second all-time leading scorer.

TORONTO
TUMBLES

JALEN ROSE PLANNED TO HELP THE RAPTORS PUT AWAY THEIR FIRST NBA CHAMPIONSHIP.

The following year, Olajuwon retired, and Carter struggled to return to form. The team received key contributions from young players such as Peterson and guard Voshon Lenard, but the Raptors labored through a difficult year, finishing 24–58. Following the season, Wilkens was fired, and Kevin O'Neill, a former assistant coach with the Pistons, was hired to lead the team.

Prior to the 2003–04 season, Toronto's general manager, Glen Grunwald, promised changes if the Raptors didn't show improvement. After an 8–8 start, Grunwald pulled the trigger on a trade that sent Davis and forwards Jerome Williams and Chris Jefferies to the Bulls for guard Jalen Rose and forwards Donyell Marshall and Lonny Baxter. Management hoped that the addition of Rose's ball-handling and Marshall's solid scoring would boost an

PLAYOFFS AT LAST

Like most expansion teams, the Toronto Raptors suffered through their share of losing seasons during the early years. In its first four seasons, Toronto never posted a winning record and never made the playoffs. But during the 1999–2000 season, the Raptors finally broke through. Combining the athleticism of young star swingmen Vince Carter and Tracy McGrady with the veteran muscle of forwards Charles Oakley and Antonio Davis, the Raptors finally posted a winning record of 45–37 and secured a spot in the playoffs. "We really owed this to the people of Toronto for sticking with us during the tough years," said head coach Butch Carter after the team clinched its first trip to the postseason. "We hope we made 'em proud." After losing the first two playoff contests on the road against New York, Toronto hoped that its fired-up home crowd would spur the team to victory, but it was not to be. The Raptors lost 87–80 and were eliminated. Despite the defeat, the 1999–2000 Raptors proved one thing—a winner could be built in Toronto.

offense that had grown stagnant. "We have to find scoring from people other than Vince Carter," said O'Neill. "The team needs more balance, and Vince needs more help."

By trading Davis, the Raptors were also able to provide more playing time for the team's first-round pick from the 2003 NBA Draft, forward Chris Bosh. Drafted after only one year at the Georgia Institute of Technology (Georgia Tech), the 6-foot-10 and 230-pound Bosh needed playing time to develop his considerable skills and gain the strength needed to battle the league's big men. While Bosh performed admirably as a rookie, averaging 11.5 points and 7.4 boards per game, the Raptors fell apart after the All-Star break, posting an 8–24 record down the stretch to finish 33–49. O'Neill was then fired, and Sam Mitchell, a former assistant with the Milwaukee Bucks, was brought in to coach the team.

Before play began for the 2004–05 season, the Eastern Conference was realigned, moving

SAM MITCHELL

COACH
RAPTORS SEASONS
2004–08

Sam Mitchell knew what it took to turn around a struggling expansion franchise. As one of the original players for the expansion Minnesota Timberwolves from 1989 to 1992 and again from 1995 to 2002, he learned the lesson that losing can be a hard habit to break if you give in to it. The tenacious Mitchell never gave in, and by the time his playing career ended in 2002, Minnesota was a consistent winner. When Mitchell became head coach of the Raptors, the franchise was suffering through a stretch of losing seasons. Few gave the first-time coach much of a chance to turn the team around, but Mitchell had faith. As a coach, his bullish, defensive-minded, and aggressive style reflected the way he had played. Slowly but surely, Mitchell transformed Toronto from a lifeless loser into one of the league's hardest-working teams. By his third season, Mitchell had led the Raptors to their first division title. "Winning is paid for with talent and effort," said Mitchell. "Talent is great, but if you don't play with heart, you aren't going anywhere."

"HE'S WORKED HARD TO DEVELOP HIS GAME, AND THIS IS HIS TEAM NOW."

— MORRIS PETERSON ON CHRIS BOSH

the Raptors to the Atlantic Division. The change did little to help the team's fortunes, however, as Toronto got off to another slow start. Frustrated by the losing, Carter asked to be traded. The struggling Raptors decided to begin rebuilding by trading their marquee star to the New Jersey Nets for center Alonzo Mourning, forwards Eric Williams and Aaron Williams, and two first-round draft picks. The deal took a bad turn for Toronto when Mourning, a seven-time All-Star, refused to report to the team. The Raptors were eventually forced to sell his contract to the Miami Heat, and without the veteran pivotman, the young, undersized Raptors struggled again. Despite the contributions of guard Rafer Alston, Rose, and Bosh, the Raptors finished 33–49 for the second straight season.

oronto's troubles continued in 2005–06. Mitchell consistently got strong efforts out of players such as guard Mike James and rookie forward Charlie Villanueva, but the team's thin bench and inexperience doomed the Raptors to a 27–55 record. One bright spot during the down year was the play of Bosh.

In his third year, the once-skinny 21-year-old had added 15 more pounds of muscle to his long frame. Bosh averaged 22.5 points and 9.2 rebounds per game, good enough to earn a spot on his first All-Star team. "When Chris first got here, he was a kid, but we needed him to play like a man," said Peterson. "Now Chris is a man. He's worked hard to develop his game, and this is his team now."

A FRUSTRATED ERIC WILLIAMS SPOKE PUBLICLY ABOUT THE RAPTORS' CHAOTIC TIMES.

STAVING OFF EXTINCTION

TORONTO LOOKED TO REBUILD WITH HELP FROM ANDREA "THE MAGICIAN" BARGNANI.

espite the rough four-year stretch, the development of Bosh gave fans hope—hope that was compounded when Toronto won the NBA Draft lottery, giving it the top overall pick in the 2006 Draft. With it, new general manager Bryan Colangelo chose forward Andrea Bargnani from Italy. The 20-year-old 7-footer had nimble feet and could shoot from all over the floor.

In the same off-season, Toronto traded Villanueva to the Bucks for point guard T. J. Ford. The speedy floor leader excelled at penetrating defenses, which made him a scoring threat and also opened up opportunities for teammates to rack up points. The Raptors felt he was an ideal candidate to wring the full potential out of Bosh and Bargnani. Toronto also signed guard Anthony Parker, who had spent several seasons playing overseas and developing into a

FORWARD HEDO TURKOGLU PLAYED IN HIS NATIVE TURKEY BEFORE JOINING THE NBA IN 2000.

solid long-range shooter and tough defender.

The roster changes proved effective that season. Bargnani and Parker kept defenses spread wide with their outside shooting, creating perfect driving opportunities for Ford, who tallied a career-high 7.9 assists per contest in 2006–07. The balanced contributions took some pressure off Bosh, who averaged 22.6 points and 10.7 rebounds per game. The Raptors soared to a 47–35 mark and captured their first Atlantic Division title. Coincidentally, in the playoffs, Toronto's opponent was the Vince Carter-led New Jersey Nets. The upstart Raptors gave the veteran Nets a tough fight, but they eventually lost the series, four games to two.

Hopes were high for Toronto in 2007–08, but injuries to Ford and Bosh limited the team's effectiveness. One bright spot was the play of guard Jose Calderon. The Spanish native

averaged 11.2 points and 8.3 assists per game and proved to be a quality starter while Ford was out. Despite Calderon's emergence, the Raptors slipped to a 41–41 record and were eliminated by the Magic in five games in the first round of the playoffs.

After constructing two semi-successful campaigns with a young club, Colangelo set Toronto back in 2008–09. Prior to the season, he dealt away Ford, massive rookie center Roy Hibbert, and two other players to acquire six-time All-Star forward Jermaine O'Neal from the Indiana Pacers. The trade was questionable not only because it cost Toronto young talent, but also because the Raptors already had the 6-foot-10 Bosh and 7-foot Bargnani at that position and seemingly had little need for the 6-foot-11 O'Neal. After an 8–9 start, Colangelo fired Coach Mitchell, but it quickly

CHRIS BOSH

POSITION FORWARD / CENTER
HEIGHT 6-FOOT-10
RAPTORS SEASONS 2003–10

One of the NBA's best young players of the 2000s, Texas native Chris Bosh quickly became the heart and soul of the Toronto Raptors. Only 19 years old when he was taken fourth overall in the 2003 NBA Draft, Bosh willingly—and admirably—battled NBA veterans 10 years older and 30 pounds heavier his rookie year, earning their respect. At 6-foot-10 and with a 7-foot-3 wingspan, Bosh's incredibly long body soon made him an excellent shot blocker and ferocious finisher around the basket. Graceful and fast for a big man, Bosh ran the floor with abandon, often punctuating fast breaks with powerful dunks. Aside from on-court performance—Bosh remained the franchise leader in points, rebounds, and blocks as of 2014—his fun-loving personality and numerous charitable works endeared him to players and fans alike. "Chris Bosh is an incredible young man," said Raptors coach Sam Mitchell. "He gives you everything he's got on the court, he inspires his teammates, and he gives back to the community. It's rare to see that kind of maturity in someone so young."

r B to 386

TORONTO
10

NBA ALL-STAR 2010

42

GUARD DeMAR DeROZAN MADE FLYING LOOK EASY AT THE 2010 SLAM DUNK CONTEST IN DALLAS.

(DUNKS) N

INTERNATIONAL RAPTORS

Basketball was once played almost exclusively in North America, but as the sport's popularity spread, talent began cropping up all over the world. By 2014, nearly 100 international players were competing in the NBA, and perhaps no team has been as welcoming to foreigners the Toronto Raptors. Since 2000, Toronto has fielded players from Argentina, Australia, Belize, Brazil, China, Croatia, Dominica, France, Hungary, Italy, Lithuania, New Zealand, Nigeria, Panama, Puerto Rico, Scotland, Senegal, Serbia, Slovenia, Spain, Turkey, and the United Kingdom. Aside from the sheer number of international players Toronto has hosted, the franchise has demonstrated a tremendous amount of faith in individual foreign stars. The Raptors became the first franchise in NBA history to select a European player with the top overall draft pick when they selected Italian forward Andrea Bargnani in 2006. "The days of the world's best basketball players coming only from the United States are long over," said Raptors general manager Bryan Colangelo after drafting Bargnani. "Toronto is an international city, and I guess it makes sense the Raptors should be an international team." Perhaps surprisingly, as of 2014, Toronto had only one Canadian-born player in its history—center Jamaal Magloire.

became apparent that coaching wasn't the only problem, as the team skidded to a 33–49 record, and O'Neal was traded away before the season even ended. Rookie guard DeMar DeRozan joined the Raptors in 2009–10 and helped boost the club to 40–42, but Toronto missed the playoffs yet again.

he club was faced with a tough decision the following off-season: it could devote a huge portion of its salary to Bosh to keep him in Toronto, or it could use the star as a bargaining chip to build for the future. Toronto chose the latter option and dealt the forward to the Heat in exchange for extra first-round picks in the 2011 Draft. Bosh's departure meant more opportunities for Bargnani, who averaged a career-high 21.4 points in 2010–11. DeRozan added 17.2 points per contest, and his fondness for powerful, high-flying finishes kept fans on the edge of their seats. Unfortunately, the team's defense was amongst the worst in the league, and the Raptors dropped to a disappointing 22–60 record. New coach Dwane Casey was brought in to shore up the defense the next year, and he was successful in that regard. Unfortunately, the offense deteriorated in the meantime, and the Raptors finished 23–43 in a lockout-shortened campaign.

To give the 2012–13 offense a jump start, Toronto brought in fast-paced point guard Kyle Lowry to team up with DeRozan and Bargnani. Despite strong individual performances from this trio, the team struggled overall, losing 19 of its first 23 games. In hopes of righting the ship, Toronto took part in a three-team trade that brought in young forward Rudy Gay. Gay boasted a solid all-around game and helped the club play tougher down the stretch, including a 7–1 finish. "This team has great bones. I've seen it," Gay said at season's end. "We have a lot of potential and have a lot of good pieces."

However, one of the biggest pieces, Bargnani, was traded away to the Knicks by new general manager Masai Ujiri in an attempt to freshen up the roster. After the Raptors got off to a slow start in 2013, a midseason blockbuster trade sent Gay to the Kings for energetic new players such as guard Greivis Vásquez. With Lowry and DeRozan leading the offense and seven-foot center Jonas Valančiūnas pulling down boards, the Raptors capped off an improved team effort by securing a spot in the playoffs for the first time since 2008. For many, the season was already a success. "These Raptors are way ahead of schedule on their rebuilding plans, have captured the attention of their fans, and are probably the best version of the team to have existed," wrote Grant Hughes on BleacherReport.com.

In 2014–15, the Raptors once again made it to the playoffs and bested their franchise record from the previous season by winning 49 games. Although they lost in the first round of the playoffs, guard Lou Williams became the first Toronto player to be honored with the Sixth Man of the Year Award at season's end. While individual stars such as Damon Stoudamire, Vince Carter, and Chris Bosh have given fans reasons to cheer throughout the years, the club overall is getting closer to fielding a contender. But just as the Canadian city began as a promising alternative to early U.S. settlements, Toronto remains eager to prove that it is second to none, and it's only a matter of time before the Raptors sink their claws into an NBA title.

DeMAR DeROZAN'S 2014 ALL-STAR SPOT GAVE RAPTORS FANS NEW REASON TO CHEER.

INDEX